Biblical Boundaries
Workbook

Esther Hosea

Copyright © 2018 Cherith Peters

All rights reserved.

No part of this book may be reproduced or transmitted in any form or by any means, except as expressly permitted in writing by the Author. Requests for permission should be addressed in writing/email to HDLD Ministries; hisdearlyloveddaughter@outlook.com.

ISBN: 9781790117277

Unless otherwise indicated, all Scripture quotations are taken from the Holy Bible, New Living Translation, copyright © 1996, 2004, 2007, 2013 by Tyndale House Foundation. Used by permission of Tyndale House Publishers, Inc., Carol Stream, Illinois 60188. All rights reserved.

Cover art photo credit – GLady, Pixabay.

HDLD Ministries
hisdearlyloveddaughter.com

CONTENTS

1	Defining Boundaries – God's Way	1
2	5 Principles We Learn About Boundaries from God's Example	9
3	5 More Principles We Learn From God's Example in Scripture	19
4	Following God's Example: 10 Guidelines Worksheet	31
5	5 Rules for Setting Boundaries Clearly Laid Out in Scripture	47
6	How do I Set Biblical Boundaries? 5 Steps to Get You Started	59
7	Setting Boundaries Worksheet	68
8	Example Worksheet	76
9	How Biblical Boundaries Put God in Control	84
10	A Prayer for Help	88

THANK-YOU to all the friends who helped me get this book through the writing and editing process. Your help was invaluable to me and I appreciate you! Special thanks to Bethany Peters and Heidi Rynders who spent a great deal of time with the material, checking and double checking it for me, and to Beka Evington who inspired me to make this into a workbook in the first place. I love you all!

Tons and tons of thanks to my wonderful husband and precious children, who have been so patient with me as my time commitments have changed so much in recent years. You all are my world, and I love you more than even I can put into words!

Finally, thanks be to God who has given His Word and the Holy Spirit to guide me in every aspect of my life. As if the undeserved privilege of salvation wasn't enough, He has showered me with grace upon grace and I will love Him for all of my days!

Notes from the Author:

I hope you enjoy this workbook on Biblical boundaries! It is my prayer that God will use it to help you discern His will in your relationships, and to better understand His heart.

Every here and there you will find sections blocked off and titled "Dig Into Scripture." These sections are sort of like bonus content. They aren't necessary in order to complete the chapter, but rather intended for those who want to go deeper into the Word of God. Some of them will take significant time to complete. Please feel the freedom to move on with the regular content of the workbook and do these sections at your own pace if doing so would be more beneficial to you. These sections are intended to enrich your experience with this content, not hinder it. So use it accordingly.

1

DEFINING BOUNDARIES
GOD'S WAY

Establishing strong, Biblical boundaries is one of the hardest, yet most important things for a betrayed wife to do. Really, it's one of the hardest, yet most important things for any believer to do. Unfortunately, it's a task that leaves most of us wondering where and how to even start. Many of us have spent our lives believing unconditional love looks different than the Bible actually describes it. We mistakenly think setting boundaries is mean, or unloving, or... gasp... un-submissive.

In fact, it is often the most loving, God-honoring thing we can do! God sets strong boundaries with us, and He makes it clear in Scripture that we are to do the same in our relationships. All of them. So, we're going to put ourselves under a microscope, and dig into Scripture to explore what the Bible has to say about boundaries, and how these things should change us. We'll learn what Biblical boundaries look like, how to set them up, and how being obedient in this area ultimately puts God in control.

Let's get to work!

------ Defining Boundaries ------

First things first, let's look at a few ways the word "boundary" has already been defined:

<u>Merriam-Webster</u>
"Something that indicates or fixes a limit or extent."
(Merriam-Webster, Incorporated, 2018)

<u>The Oxford English Dictionary</u>
"A line which marks the limits of an area; a dividing line."
(Oxford University Press, 2018)

I kinda like both. When we set personal boundaries, we're 'drawing a line' or 'fixing a limit.' We're clearly communicating where the actions of another will reach the extent of our tolerance and thus divide them from us. Boundaries define our borders; who we are, where we begin and where we end.

Do the people in your life know where your borders are? Do you?

_____

_____

PERSONAL BOUNDARIES DRAW A LINE OR FIX A LIMIT. THEY CLEARLY COMMUNICATE WHERE THE ACTIONS OF ANOTHER WILL REACH THE EXTENT OF OUR TOLERANCE AND THUS DIVIDE THEM FROM US. THEY DEFINE OUR BORDERS; WHO WE ARE, WHERE WE BEGIN AND WHERE WE END.

------ Why Boundaries are Important ------

A person with no boundaries is a person who is undefined and unprotected. This opens us up to unnecessary danger, and will most often result in confusion - both on the part of those we find ourselves in relationship with, and within ourselves. We won't know how to proceed when we feel violated, because we won't know for sure that we HAVE been violated.

Have you ever found yourself confused about whether or not a person had crossed a line in how he/she treated you?

_____

_____

What do you think was at the root of that confusion?

_____

_____

_____

Let's think about this in terms of a piece of land. If we found ourselves in a situation in which we owned a valuable estate, but had neighbors who had no respect for our property, what could we do? Do we have a right to expect them not to violate what belongs to us?

I think we all know we do have that right, according to the law. The thing is, we can't "make" people obey the law can we? In that situation we could go to our neighbors and let them know our expectations, but if they refuse to cooperate we have to make some choices.

Likely the first thing we'd try would be to build a fence. The fence still doesn't control them. It can't. But it does clearly establish where the line is and when they've crossed it.

We could then communicate to them that if they crossed that border again, we'd have to bring in law enforcement. Again, they still have the ability to cross over onto our property and do their damage, and we've left that decision to them. However, if they made the choice to come onto our property, we would call the police, and we'd press charges.

This wouldn't make us mean people. We did everything we could to prevent that course of action. But the neighbors refused to respect our boundaries, so they chose to bring down the penalties of the law. Not us.

Personal boundaries are no different.

------ Boundaries and the Bible ------

Would it surprise you to discover the Bible says believers can, and even should expect other believers to live up to a Biblical standard of respect? Would it surprise you to find that we're meant to have confidence in our principles, and hold others to those standards as well? My hope is that by the time you've finished this workbook, you'll be able to live in that freedom.

Titus 2:14-15 – He gave His life to free us from every kind of sin, to cleanse us, and to make us His very own people, totally committed to doing good deeds. You must teach these things and encourage the believer to do them. You have the authority to correct them when necessary, so don't let anyone disregard what you say.

I struggled with the idea of boundaries for many years! A combination of my own personal baggage, and a misunderstanding of unconditional love caused me to be torn between knowing I couldn't, and shouldn't tolerate my husband's sin, and believing that taking any kind of action would be selfish and unloving. I wrestled with it for years. Each time a new discovery of his acting out would come to light I would feel so helpless. I would clearly communicate to him that it wasn't okay, but beyond that, I just didn't know what to do.

Since then I've learned that just as a soundly built wall protects everything within, or a clearly marked property line plainly establishes when an individual has crossed over and violated our property, a clearly defined personal boundary will do the same things for our hearts. It will protect us, and when we're inevitably violated, we won't have to explain why or how because it will be clearly evident by which side of the fence the person is standing on!

> What has caused you to struggle with the idea of personal boundaries in the past?
>
> _____
>
> _____
>
> What has stopped you from setting them for yourself?
>
> _____
>
> _____

Boundaries are a necessary part of every human relationship. Parents need to establish clear and concise boundaries for their children. Employers need to do the same for their employees, and vice-versa. Friendships need boundaries. Families need boundaries. Church bodies need boundaries within their members. Marriages desperately need boundaries. In fact, even our relationship with God has been established upon clearly communicated boundaries from Him to us.

That's right! Our God is a God of boundaries. He established them. He communicated them. He keeps them. And He commands us to do the same!

------ A God of Boundaries ------

As I've been reading the Bible over the last few years, specifically looking for examples of God's boundaries, I've been blown away! In fact, I challenge you to find a single book of the Bible that doesn't include a boundary! Whether they are physical, emotional, spiritual or relational. Even creation itself demonstrates His power to define the lines between heaven and earth, land and sea, Creator and created.

DIG INTO SCRIPTURE

Find an example of God's use of each kind of boundary from the Bible

Physical (ex. Prov. 8:39) -

Emotional (ex. Deut. 6:5) -

Spiritual (ex. Ex. 20:5) -

Relational (ex. Lev. 26) -

Additionally, our God is a covenant maker, and covenants are basically clearly defined and agreed upon boundaries. From the beginning of Genesis to the end of Revelation God lays out His parameters for His people.

> In each of the following verses, underline the boundary God lays down, and circle the consequence He establishes for a violation.

Genesis 2:15-17
The Lord God placed the man in the Garden of Eden to tend and watch over it. But the Lord God warned him, "You may freely eat the fruit of every tree in the garden – except the tree of the knowledge of good and evil. If you eat its fruit, you are sure to die."

Revelation 22:11-15
Let the one who is doing harm continue to do harm; let the one who is vile continue to be vile; let the one who is righteous continue to live righteously; let the one who is holy continue to be holy.
"Look, I am coming soon, bringing my reward with me to repay all people according to their deeds. I am the Alpha and the Omega, the First and the Last, the Beginning and the End."
Blessed are those who wash their robes. They will be permitted to enter through the gates of the city and eat the fruit from the tree of life. Outside the city are the dogs – the sorcerers, the sexually immoral, the murderers, the idol worshipers, and all who love to live a lie.

You see, right from the beginning God gave Adam his limits. He told him what he could do, what he couldn't do, and what would happen if he did it anyhow. And all the way to the very end, God has clearly established His borders and plainly defined who will be allowed inside of them, and who will not. Our God is, without question, a God of boundaries!

So, let's see what we can learn from Him, shall we? Let's examine some of His boundaries and see if we can gain some understanding of our Father's heart. After all, we want to be like Him

2

5 PRINCIPLES WE LEARN ABOUT BOUNDARIES FROM GOD'S EXAMPLE

------ Principle 1 ------

Healthy boundaries stem from an understanding of who we are, and a refusal to be defined as anything less.

Jeremiah 5:22-23 & 25
Have you no respect for me? Why don't you tremble in My presence? I, the Lord, define the ocean's sandy shoreline and an everlasting boundary that the waters cannot cross. The waves may toss and roar, but they can never pass the boundaries I set. But My people have stubborn and rebellious hearts. They have turned away and abandoned Me... Your wickedness has deprived you of these wonderful blessings. Your sin has robbed you of all these good things.

God knows who He is – He is God. He doesn't pretend to be anything less, and He does not tolerate being treated as such. He has no qualms about boldly declaring His Lordship, no fear of claiming His attributes. So many of the boundaries He has established stem from this simple truth – Disrespecting Him as anything less than the One True God will deprive us of blessing, rob us of good things, and separate us from Him.

We need to follow His example. We need to know and understand who we are in Him. The children of the One True God are set apart. They do not abide with sin or join themselves to corruption. They establish their borders with integrity, only allowing in what honors Him, and therefore respects their position in Him.

In the verse below: underline everything that reveals your identity. Circle every boundary (limits you should set) that should result from that identity.

2 Corinthians 6:14-18

Don't team up with those who are unbelievers. How can righteousness be a partner with wickedness? How can light live with darkness? What harmony can there be between Christ and the devil? How can a believer be a partner with an unbeliever? And what union can there be between God's temple and idols? For we are the temple of the living God. As God said: "I will live in them and walk among them. I will be their God and they will be My people. Therefore, come out from among unbelievers, and separate yourselves from them, says the Lord. Don't touch their filthy things, and I will welcome you. And I will be your Father, and you will be My sons and daughters, says the Lord Almighty."

Do you think you define yourself the way God defines you? Why, or why not?

_____

_____

_____

DIG INTO SCRIPTURE

Read the whole book of Ephesians and write down some things you learn about your identity in Christ.

_____
_____
_____
_____
_____
_____
_____
_____
_____
_____
_____
_____
_____
_____
_____

What are just a few implications you can think of that these truths about your identity should have on where your boundaries should fall?

_____
_____
_____
_____
_____
_____
_____
_____

------ Principle 2 ------

Biblical boundaries are made with the intent to draw others in and build healthy relationships. They are not meant to tear them down or punish.

Acts 17:26-27
From one man He created all the nations throughout the whole earth. He decided beforehand when they should rise and fall, and He determined their boundaries. His purpose was for the nations to seek after God and perhaps feel their way toward Him and find Him – though He is not far from any one of us.

Everything God has established, every perimeter He lays is meant to draw all people everywhere to Him. Even the consequences of broken boundaries have been established, not simply to punish, but to bring us to the realization that we need Him - desperately. If going it alone led to comfort and contentment, what would compel us to seek reconciliation to Him?

Our boundaries – if they are Biblical and healthy will do the same. If we go out of our way to make a person who is violating our borders comfortable, we are doing him a great disservice! We're enabling him to continue to live in sin, or even making it easy to do so.

Well-crafted consequences, on the other hand, carry with them the longing to draw others back into right relationship. They aren't meant to make them suffer for the sake of suffering, but to help them recognize the pain and displeasure of living in sin, and the peace and joy of right living.

> Can you think of a time when a consequence drew you closer to God?
>
> _____

------ Principle 3 ------
Healthy boundaries lovingly offer a choice to others rather than attempting to control them.

Revelation 3:20-22
Look! I stand at the door and knock. If you hear my voice and open the door, I will come in, and we will share a meal together as friends. Those who are victorious will sit with Me on My throne, just as I was victorious and sat with my Father on His throne. Anyone with ears to hear must listen to the Spirit and understand what He is saying to the churches.

Scripture is clear. God does not force us into relationship with Him. He could. He has the power to. He *wants* us to come to Him. We're told that He is not willing that any should perish, but that all should come to repentance. Yet, He doesn't force His way in. He stands at the door and knocks. He invites us to choose Him and rewards us greatly when we do.

Have you ever thought of boundaries as a way to control someone else? What do you think made you think of them that way instead of how the Bible demonstrates them here?

_____

_____

_____

Healthy, Biblical boundaries follow God's example. He has the right to force us to follow Him, just as we have "the right" to a healthy relationship with certain people: a child, a parent, or especially a spouse. When My Love promised to spend the rest of his life loving, honoring, and cherishing me, he gave me the right to demand that.

Healthy boundaries say, "I may have the right to this, but I'm still going to let you choose. I'll invite you to love, honor and cherish me, but you get to choose whether you will. You get to choose whether you'll experience the rewards of a relationship with me or choose instead to cross the line and give up a relationship with me."

Remember, God doesn't come in to enjoy a meal of friendship with those who leave the door unanswered. Those who reject Him will not sit with Him on His throne. They were given the choice and they chose separation from Him.

DIG INTO SCRIPTURE

Read each of the following Scripture passages:

- Genesis 6:5-8
- Deuteronomy 32:15-21
- Ezekiel 6:8-10
- Romans 2:6-9
- John 3:18-19
- 1 Samuel 15:33
- 2 Chronicles 7:19-20

How does it make you feel to realize how many times God has been rejected as a result of establishing boundaries and sticking to them?

_____
_____
_____

Does it comfort you to know God understands rejection?

_____
_____

------ **Principle 4** ------

Biblical boundaries clearly communicate their expectations and the reasons behind them.

Deuteronomy 7: 1-4
When the Lord your God brings you into the land you are about to enter and occupy, He will clear away many nations ahead of you...when the Lord your God hands these nations over to you and you conquer them, you must completely destroy them. Make no treaties with them and show them no mercy. You must not intermarry with them. Do not let your daughters and sons marry their sons and daughters, for they will lead your children away from me to worship other gods. Then the anger of the Lord will burn against you, and He will quickly destroy you.

> In the verses above, underline the expectation (or boundary) God had for His people. Circle His reason. Now draw a square around the consequence that would result from a violation.

God does not make His people guess what He expects of them. He doesn't assume that they'll just know. He also rarely demands something without explaining why. Instead, He lays out His expectations in detail, communicates them clearly (almost always more than once), explains His reasoning and motivation, and very often asks that the boundary be written down and regularly reviewed.

A healthy Biblical boundary will follow this example. When making healthy boundaries, we'll take the time to examine our motives so we'll be able to clearly communicate them. We will sit down with our relationship partner (husband, child, parent, etc....) and have a conversation about the boundary and the reasons behind it. (If he/she won't listen, we'll write it down or record it clearly and in detail and ask him to read it or listen to it.) If we need to do it again later, we will. Once the boundary has been clearly communicated we'll write it down and ask that it be confirmed. We'll leave no room for there to be any confusion by us or anyone else what is expected.

What are some things that have stood in the way of you establishing clearly communicated boundaries in the past?

_____

_____

_____

What are some solutions to eliminate those obstacles?

_____

_____

_____

------ Principle 5 ------
Healthy boundaries clearly define the consequences of a violation of their borders.

Romans 6:23
For the wages of sin is death, but the free gift of God is eternal life through Christ Jesus our Lord.

Exodus 19:12
Mark off a boundary all around the mountain. Warn the people, "Be careful! Do not go up on the mountain or even touch its boundaries. Anyone who touches the mountain will certainly be put to death."

God never minces words when it comes to letting us know what will happen if we choose to step outside of His boundaries. He made it clear to Adam and Eve in the garden, He stated it plainly to Abraham, Isaac, Jacob, Moses, David, and countless others in the Old Testament, and He has communicated it clearly to us in this New Testament age.

The wages of sin is, always has been, and always will be death. Eternal separation from Him. Period. The only way to avoid those consequences is to operate within His boundaries – to accept His free gift of saving grace and eternal life in relationship with Him.

Healthy boundaries will always be clear about what will happen outside of their borders. This is the only way the person in relationship with us can have all the information necessary to make his choice.

Adam and Eve chose knowledge over perfection. The people of Israel chose indulgence in the worship of foreign gods made of wood and stone over submission to the One who chose them and rescued them and offered them His favor. People far too often choose the pain of violated boundaries over healthy relationship. This is true for God, and sadly, it will be true for us too. Boundaries don't ensure that there is no violation. They simply lay out what will happen as a result.

Take some time to journal your thoughts so far when it comes to biblical boundaries. What have you learned? What scares you? What have you done right in the past, and what have you done wrong? How do you think these principles might help you?

_____
_____
_____
_____

3

5 MORE PRINCIPLES WE LEARN FROM GOD'S EXAMPLE IN SCRIPTURE

Let's review. So far we've established that healthy, biblical boundaries which follow the example set by God in Scripture:

1. Stem from an understanding of who we are, and a refusal to be defined as anything less.
2. Are made with the intent to draw others in and build healthy relationships, not tear them down or punish.
3. Lovingly offer choice to others rather than attempting to control them.
4. Clearly communicate their expectations, and the reasons behind them.
5. Clearly define the consequences of a violation of their borders.

Let's continue our list with 5 more principles about healthy boundaries clearly demonstrated by God in the Bible.

------ Principle 6 ------
Biblical boundaries will draw out the true heart of others, ultimately expediting a resolution – one way or the other.

Matthew 19:16-22
Someone came to Jesus with this question: "Teacher, what good deed must I do to have eternal life?"
"Why ask Me about what is good?" Jesus replied. "There is only One who is good. But to answer your question – if you want to receive eternal life, keep the commandments."
"Which ones?" The man asked. And Jesus replied: "You must not murder. You must not commit adultery. You must not steal. You must not testify falsely. Honor your father and mother. Love your neighbor as yourself."
"I've obeyed all these commandments," the young man replied. "What else must I do?"
Jesus told him, "If you want to be perfect, go and sell all your possessions and give the money to the poor, and you will have treasure in heaven. Then come, follow Me."
But when the young man heard this, he went away sad, for he had many possessions.

We can't see the heart of another, as Jesus could. He already knew this man was not ready to humble himself and give up everything for the Kingdom of God. The boundary He established here (go sell all your possessions and give the money to the poor) brought quickly to light what was already in the man's heart: An unwillingness to give up his possessions in order to store up treasure in heaven. Or, more accurately, a connection to the temporal that refused to look to the eternal.

Translation: He'd rather keep his stuff than follow Jesus.

Jesus could have invited the man to follow without setting this boundary (after all we don't have record of Him asking anyone else to do this), but it wouldn't have changed anything other than time. Eventually, the hardness of the man's heart would still have come to light, and he still would have chosen his things over Jesus. Drawing the line right away simply saved both Jesus and the man from wasting their time, energy, and emotions on a lie.

It's time to do some hard self-evaluation. Have you refrained from setting much needed boundaries because you're afraid doing so will result in an end to the relationship?

_____

_____

Do you often hold back from dealing with a situation the way you believe it should be dealt with because you're afraid of how your relationship partner will react?

_____

_____

What do you think will happen in the long-run as a result of these decisions? Will it really ever make anything better?

_____

_____

_____

_____

Often times, we're afraid to enact boundaries because we fear that doing so will result in the loss of a relationship we desperately want to keep intact. But the reality is, we're being shortsighted and un-trusting (of God's sovereignty) when we allow this to stop us from being obedient. Strong, Biblical boundaries save us from spending years being hurt again and again by a fake relationship. A lie.

And remember, the story is never over until it's over. Just because this man walked away on that day doesn't mean he never came back. The Bible doesn't tell us. He may have! Just because our boundaries escalate a situation today, doesn't mean the person or the relationship is lost forever. GOD IS IN CONTROL – trust Him!

DIG INTO SCRIPTURE

Read Psalm 37 in at least the NLT version and the ESV version. Take your time with the passage. Meditate on its promises, then write out what you hear God telling you through it.

_____

_____

_____

_____

_____

What do you see in the passage that specifically speaks to God's sovereignty? Do you feel like you can trust Him with your future? Why or why not?

_____

_____

_____

_____

_____

_____

------ Principle 7 ------
Biblical boundaries are genuinely concerned for the well-being of another.

Genesis 4:6-7
"Why are you so angry?" The Lord asked Cain. "Why do you look so dejected? You will be accepted if you do what is right. But if you refuse to do what is right, then watch out! Sin is crouching at the door, eager to control you. But you must subdue it and be its master."

Deuteronomy 8:5-6
Think about it: Just as a parent disciplines a child, the Lord your God disciplines you for your own good. So obey the commands of the Lord your God by walking in His ways and fearing Him.

God does not silently leave us with the unchecked freedom to do whatever we want because God cares too much about our well-being to do so. Just as we don't allow our 2-year-old child to play with sharp knives (a boundary!), not because we want to deprive her of fun, but because we don't want her to get hurt by something she absolutely cannot handle.

Does it seem mean to you for a parent to make a boundary for her child that doesn't allow her to play with knives? _____
Does it seem mean to you for a wife to make a boundary for her sex addicted husband that doesn't allow him to access the internet in private? _____
If your answers aren't the same, why do you think that is?

_____

Biblical boundaries understand the dangers and vulnerabilities of unchecked borders. When we're truly concerned for the well-being of those we love, we will establish guidelines to help keep them (and us) safe. We will understand that sin is crouching at their door, eager to control them. We'll do everything we can to help them and protect them from it.

> Heart check time: Can you honestly say your motivation in wanting to establish strong boundaries is rooted in a sincere desire to do what is best for the other person? If so, great! But if not, take a minute to pray right now and ask God to purify your heart and align your motives with His.

------ Principle 8 ------
Biblical boundaries are loving.

Proverbs 23:13-14
Don't fail to discipline your children. The rod of punishment won't kill them. Physical discipline may well save them from death.

Proverbs 3:11-12
My child, don't reject the Lord's discipline, and don't be upset when He corrects you. For the Lord corrects those He loves, just as a father corrects the child in whom he delights.

This is probably the part about boundaries that I struggle with the most. It doesn't "feel" loving to say, "If you do x, I will have to ask you to leave our house for 90 days." It feels mean.

The thing is, I can see it easily with my children. I totally get that setting strong boundaries with them and enforcing painful consequences when they disobey is a loving way to set them up for success in life. I can understand that as a result of my delight in them, I will faithfully discipline and correct.

But my husband is not my child. My friends, my parents, extended family members… These people are not the same as my children. Sometimes it doesn't feel like I have a right to "discipline" those people.

Then I read a passage like 1 Corinthians 5:

> I can hardly believe the report about the sexual immorality going on among you – something that even pagans don't do. I am told that a man in your church is living in sin with his stepmother. You are so proud of yourselves, but you should be mourning in sorrow and shame. And you should remove this man from among your fellowship.
> Even though I am not with you in person, I am with you in the Spirit. And as though I were there, I have already passed judgement on this man in the name of the Lord Jesus. You must call a meeting of the church. I will be present with you in spirit, and so will the power of our Lord Jesus. Then you must throw this man out and hand him over to Satan so that his sinful nature will be destroyed and he himself will be saved on the day the Lord returns.
> Your boasting on this is terrible. Don't you realize that this sin is like a little yeast that spreads through the whole batch of dough? Get rid of the old "yeast" by removing this wicked person from among you. Then you will be like a fresh batch of dough made without yeast, which is what you really are. Christ, our Passover Lamb, has been sacrificed for us. So let us celebrate the festival, not with the old bread of wickedness and evil, but with the new bread of sincerity and truth.
> When I wrote to you before, I told you not to associate with people who indulge in sexual sin. But I wasn't talking about unbelievers who indulge in sexual sin, or are greedy, or cheat people, or worship idols. You would have to leave this world to avoid people like that. I meant that you are not to associate with anyone who claims to be a believer yet indulges in sexual sin, or is greedy, or worships idols, or is abusive, or is a drunkard,

> *or cheats people. Don't even eat with such people.*
> *It isn't my responsibility to judge outsiders, but it certainly is your responsibility to judge those inside the church who are sinning. God will judge those on the outside; but as the Scriptures say, "You must remove the evil person from among you."*

Wow! You guys, God has commanded us to establish and enforce boundaries around morality with all those who claim to be believers!

Why? As an act of love.

Verse 5 shows us that disciplining such violations will basically force the person to hit rock bottom, which is the most likely way to see him restored.

If we love our fellow believers, we will enact the "rod of punishment" as Proverbs 23 describes it. Because doing so won't kill them, but it may well save them from death!

DIG INTO SCRIPTURE
Read the following passages from the Old Testament:
-Leviticus 20   -Ezra 9   -Deuteronomy 32:1-47

Take note of how the Lord wanted His people to be set apart. Jot down His instructions for removing evil from among the people. What was the consequence of not following God's instructions to remove the evil people? How should this example warn us to take 1 Corinthians 5 seriously?

_____
_____
_____
_____
_____

------ Principle 9 ------
Biblical boundaries are faithfully enforced – even though it really hurts us to do so.

Genesis 6:5-7
The Lord observed the extent of human wickedness on the earth, and He saw that everything they thought or imagines was consistently and totally evil. So the Lord was sorry He had ever made them and put them on the earth. It broke His heart. And the Lord said, "I will wipe this human race I have created from the face of the earth...

Romans 1:18-32
But God shows His anger from heaven against all sinful, wicked people who suppress the truth by their wickedness. They know the truth about God because He has made it obvious to them... Yes, they knew God, but they wouldn't worship Him as God or even give Him thanks. And they began to think up foolish ideas of what God was like. As a result, their minds became dark and confused. Claiming to be wise, they instead became utter fools. And instead of worshiping the glorious, ever-living God, they worshiped idols made to look like mere people and birds and animals and reptiles. So God abandoned them to do whatever shameful things their hearts desired...They traded the truth about God for a lie. So they worshiped and served the things God created instead of the Creator Himself, who is worthy of eternal praise! Amen. That is why God abandoned them to their shameful desires... Since they thought it foolish to acknowledge God, He abandoned them to their foolish thinking and let them do things that should never be done. Their lives became full of every kind of wickedness, sin, greed, hate, envy, murder, quarreling, deception, malicious behavior, and gossip...

The Bible makes it clear that the sin of human beings breaks God's heart. He loves us - dearly. But when we abandon Him – when we choose to live according to our own fleshly desires instead of according to His commands - He will enforce His boundaries, though it breaks His heart to do so. He will leave us to our folly.

We should follow His example. When those we love (dearly) abandon a life of integrity, it is imperative for the good of every single person involved that we hold to our boundaries. We must draw lines that separate us from their foolishness and sin, lest we reap the consequences too!

> Have you ever had to deal with the consequences of another person's sin? _____
>
> How would a well designed boundary protect you from that scenario in the future? _____
>
> How might that same boundary actually protect the other person as well? _____
>
> What's holding you back from setting a boundary to protect both you and the person you love? Is it fear of the pain it will cause you to do it? _____
>
> What do you think God wants you to do? _____

------ Principle 10 ------
Biblical boundaries provide a gate.

1 John 1:5-9
This is the message we heard from Jesus and now declare to you: God is light, and there is no darkness in Him at all. So we are lying if we say we have fellowship with God but go on living in spiritual darkness; we are not practicing truth. But if we are living in the light, as God is in the light, then we have fellowship with each other, and the blood of Jesus, His Son, cleanses us from all sin. If we claim we have no sin, we are only fooling ourselves and not living in the truth. But if we confess our sins to Him, He is faithful and just to forgive us our sins and to cleanse us from all wickedness.

God's boundaries are strong. They are immovable. BUT, they have a gate - a way in, and a way out.

In His infinite love, God provided a way for those who found themselves outside His borders (all of us!) to be allowed back in. He gave up His own rights and took our punishment upon Himself so that all we have to do is repent of our evil ways, turn to Him, and receive forgiveness.

We can't get inside His territory by any way other than that gate, though. He made His boundaries clear and He made ONE WAY back in: Jesus Christ! There is no other name under heaven by which we must be saved (Acts 4:12)!

Strong, healthy, Biblical boundaries will do the same. If we seek to live in obedience to Scripture, we will be willing to open our gates, give up our rights, and provide a way for one who is repentant to come back inside our borders.

> Take a minute to thank God for providing Jesus to give us a way back! Can you imagine the hopelessness of a life without a Gate?
>
> Now, take some time to meditate on your own tendency to violate God's boundaries. We are all prone to wander. The sting of betrayal has a way of opening our eyes to the pain we've caused our Savior. Take some time to sincerely apologize to God for the countless times you've broken His heart.
>
> Finally, acknowledge God's understanding of your situation and ask Him to help you navigate the treacherous waters ahead. Ask Him to give you wisdom as you think through the boundaries you need to make in your relationship. Ask Him to lead you according to His will, and thank Him for never leaving you or forsaking you!
>
> Journal any thoughts you have at this point_____
> _____
> _____
> _____
> _____
> _____
> _____
> _____
> _____
> _____
> _____
> _____
> _____
> _____
> _____
> _____

- -

We've looked at 10 principles that guide the way our Lord creates, communicates, and enforces boundaries with us. We are His children, and we are called to follow His example. May we take it seriously!

Ephesians 5:1-5
Imitate God, therefore, in everything you do, because you are His dear children. Live a life filled with love, following the example of Christ. He loved us and offered Himself as a sacrifice for us, a pleasing aroma to God.
Let there be no sexual immorality, impurity, or greed among you. Such sins have no place among God's people. Obscene stories, foolish talk, and coarse jokes – these are not for you. Instead, let there be thankfulness to God. You can be sure that no immoral, impure, or greedy person will inherit the Kingdom of Christ and of God. For a greedy person is an idolater, worshiping the things of this world.

4

FOLLOWING GOD'S EXAMPLE 10 GUIDELINES WORKSHEET

------ Principle 1 ------

Healthy boundaries stem from an understanding of who we are, and a refusal to be defined as anything less.

With as much honesty as you can muster, describe how **you believe** the people in your life would describe you:

Spouse:_____

_____

_____

_____

_____

Parents:_____

_____

_____

_____

Children:_____

_____

_____

_____

Friends:_____

_____

_____

_____

What is your own personal identity? How do you define yourself?

_____

_____

_____

_____

_____

_____

How do you believe God defines you?

_____

_____

_____

_____

_____

Dig into Scripture and find as many verses as you can that speak to your identity in Christ. (A good way to do this is to Google "verses about my identity in Christ" and use the openbible.com, and biblestudytools.com results.) Note the references that speak to your heart.

_____
_____
_____
_____

How do these verses support what you wrote about your identity?

_____
_____
_____
_____
_____

How do they contradict what you wrote about your identity?

_____
_____
_____
_____
_____
_____
_____

According to the Bible, how does God ACTUALLY define you?

___

What are the implications of this identity when it comes to relationships and setting boundaries?

___

> GOD KNOWS WHO HE IS – HE IS GOD. DISRESPECTING HIM AS ANYTHING LESS WILL DEPRIVE US OF BLESSING, ROB US OF GOOD THINGS, AND SEPARATE US FROM HIM. WE NEED TO FOLLOW HIS EXAMPLE. THE CHILDREN OF THE ONE TRUE GOD ARE SET APART. THEY DO NOT ABIDE WITH SIN OR JOIN THEMSELVES TO CORRUPTION.

------ **Principle 2** ------

Biblical boundaries are made with the intent to draw others in and build healthy relationships. They are not meant to tear them down or punish.

What would a healthy, God-honoring relationship look like to you?

_____

_____

_____

_____

Dig into Scripture and find some verses that describe a healthy relationship according to God. Note their references:

_____

_____

What is missing from your relationship that keeps it from lining up with Scripture and therefore being God-honoring?

You:_____

_____

_____

_____

Partner:_____

_____

_____

_____

What boundaries do you need to set with yourself to do a better job of fulfilling YOUR role in the relationship in a God-honoring way?

_____
_____
_____
_____

What boundaries could you set with your spouse (or parent, child, or other relationship partner) to draw him into a more healthy understanding of his role in the relationship?

_____
_____
_____
_____
_____
_____
_____

> EVERY PERIMETER GOD LAYS IS MEANT TO DRAW US TO HIM. OUR BOUNDARIES WILL DO THE SAME. WELL-CRAFTED CONSEQUENCES AREN'T MEANT TO MAKE OTHERS SUFFER FOR THE SAKE OF SUFFERING, BUT TO HELP THEM RECOGNIZE THE PAIN AND DISPLEASURE OF LIVING IN SIN, AND THE PEACE AND PLEASURE OF RIGHT LIIVING.

------ Principle 3 ------
Healthy boundaries lovingly offer choice to others rather than attempting to control them.

What is the difference between a boundary that is meant to control another person, and one that simply offers them choice?

Control:_____
_____
_____

Choice:_____
_____
_____

List some issues in your relationship that make you feel unsafe or violated:_____
_____
_____
_____

What boundaries could you set up around those specific issues that would be aimed at controlling?
_____
_____
_____
_____
_____

What are some boundaries you could set up that would instead set up a protective barrier around you and allow others a choice to either keep you safe, or stay outside that barrier?

___

How could you clearly communicate this **choice** so that it is clear this is not about control, but about protecting yourself?

___

HEALTHY BOUNDARIES SAY, "I MAY HAVE THE RIGHT TO THIS, BUT I'M STILL GOING TO LET YOU CHOOSE. I'LL INVITE YOU TO LOVE, HONOR, AND CHERISH ME, BUT YOU GET TO CHOOSE WHETHER YOU WILL. YOU GET TO CHOOSE WHETHER YOU'LL EXPERIENCE THE REWARDS OF A RELATIONSHIP WITH ME OR CHOOSE INSTEAD TO CROSS THE LINE AND GIVE UP A RELATIONSHIP WITH ME."

------ **Principle 4** ------
Biblical boundaries clearly communicate their expectations
and the reasons behind them.

Describe your communication skills in your relationship. (Just you.)

_____

_____

_____

_____

GOD DOES NOT MAKE HIS PEOPLE
GUESS WHAT HE EXPECTS OF THEM. HE
DOESN'T ASSUME THEY'LL JUST KNOW.
HE LAYS OUT HIS EXPECTATIONS IN
DETAIL, COMMUNICATES THEM
CLEARLY, EXPLAINS HIS MOTIVATION,
AND HAS THE BOUNDARY WRITTEN
DOWN. A HEALTHY BIBLICAL BOUNDARY
WILL FOLLOW HIS EXAMPLE.

What do you need to do to be more in line with God's heart when it comes to communication in your relationships?

_____

_____

_____

_____

Have you allowed the fear of another person's reactions to stop you from obedience when it comes to communication? _____

How can you practice choosing obedience and trusting God to handle the outcome?

_____

_____

_____

_____

------ Principle 5 ------
Healthy boundaries clearly define the consequences of a violation of their borders.

Part of establishing healthy, biblical boundaries is making sure the consequences we come up with for each boundary violation are appropriate, and enforceable. There's no point in communicating a boundary we're not going to have the courage to keep.

The best consequences for violated boundaries are ones that reinforce the natural consequences of the offending behavior. (For instance, if a child refuses to do her homework, the natural consequence would be that she will fail the class and have to repeat it.) We simply choose not to bail the violator out of those consequences.

Look back at the list you made under Principle 3 of issues in your relationship that make you feel unsafe, and the boundaries you could make to offer choice to your partner.

What are some simple, appropriate consequences for a violation of those boundaries that you have the power and courage to actually see through?

___

> GOD NEVER MINCES WORDS WHEN IT COMES TO LETTING US KNOW WHAT WILL HAPPEN IF WE CHOOSE TO STEP OUTSIDE OF HIS BOUNDARIES. HEALTHY BOUNDARIES WILL ALWAYS BE CLEAR ABOUT WHAT WILL HAPPEN OUTSIDE OF THEIR BORDERS. ANY OTHER SCENARIO DOES NOT OFFER THE NECESSARY INFORMATION FOR THE PERSON MAKING THE CHOICE.

How can you communicate these consequences clearly?

___

------ Principle 6 ------

Biblical boundaries will draw out the true heart of others, ultimately expediting a resolution – one way or the other.

With all you've learned about the heart of Biblical boundaries, and the heart of the One who asks us to make them, what are some steps you can take to practice obedience when it comes to trusting God with your future?

_____
_____
_____
_____

OFTENTIMES WE'RE AFRAID TO ENACT BOUNDARIES BECAUSE WE FEAR THAT DOING SO WILL RESULT IN THE LOSS OF A RELATIONSHIP WE DESPERATELY WANT TO KEEP INTACT.
THE REALITY IS, WHEN WE ALLOW THAT FEAR TO KEEP US FROM OBEDIENCE, WE'RE BEING SHORTSIGHTED AND UNTRUSTING OF GOD AND HIS SOVEREIGNTY.

What boundary is He asking you to make to leave the future in His hands?_____
_____

------ **Principle 7** ------

Biblical boundaries are genuinely concerned for the well-being of another.

How are the problem issues you listed before harming not only you, but your relationship partner?

_____
_____
_____
_____

Can you see how strong Biblical boundaries might be able to help him? _____

GOD DOES NOT SILENTLY LEAVE US WITH THE UNCHECKED FREEDOM TO DO WHATEVER WE WANT BECAUSE GOD CARES TOO MUCH ABOUT OUR OWN WELL-BEING TO DO SO. WHEN WE ARE TRULY CONCERNED FOR THOSE WE LOVE, WE WILL ESTABLISH GUIDELINES TO HELP KEEP THEM, AND US SAFE.

Does your love for your spouse (or other relationship) outweigh your fear of him? Are you willing to do what might make him angry in order to help him be the best version of himself?_____

Principle 8
Biblical boundaries are loving.

Describe what you think of when you think of Biblical love:

_____
_____
_____
_____

Knowing that GOD IS LOVE, and based on what you've learned about God in this study so far, how has your perception of Biblical love maybe been a little off?

_____
_____
_____
_____

> IF WE LOVE OUR FELLOW BELIEVERS WE WILL ENACT THE "ROD OF DISCIPLINE" BECAUSE DOING SO WON'T KILL THEM, BUT IT MAY WELL SAVE THEM FROM DEATH.

Look at Romans 12:9-10. What does sincere love do to evil? What does it cling to? _____

------ Principle 9 ------
Biblical boundaries are faithfully enforced – even though it really hurts us to do so.

What is your biggest fear when it comes to setting boundaries in your relationships?

_____

_____

How has your broken heart gotten in the way of your ability to approach your relationships in a healthy, God-honoring way?

_____

_____

_____

What can you do to take a step of faith toward God today and work on trusting Him in obedience?

_____

_____

THE SIN OF HUMAN BEINGS BREAKS GOD'S HEART. HE LOVES US. DEARLY. BUT WHEN WE ABANDON HIM AND CHOOSE TO LIVE ACCORDING TO OUR FLESH HE WILL ENFORCE HIS BOUNDARIES. EVEN THOUGH DOING SO BREAKS HIS HEART.

------ Principle 10 ------
Biblical boundaries provide a gate.

What does a gate look like in your relationship? How can you be sure to provide a way back in if there is genuine repentance?

_____
_____
_____

How might you be tempted to open the gate at the wrong times?

_____
_____

What can you do to be sure there is only one way back in and it is clearly marked? _____

> IN HIS INFINITE LOVE, GOD PROVIDED A WAY FOR THOSE WHO FOUND THEMSELVES OUTSIDE HIS BORDERS (ALL OF US) TO BE ALLOWED BACK IN. IF WE SEEK TO LIVE IN OBEDIENCE TO SCRIPTURE, WE WILL BE WILLING TO OPEN OUR GATES, GIVE UP OUR RIGHTS, AND PROVIDE A WAY FOR ONE WHO IS REPENTANT TO COME BACK INSIDE OUR BORDERS.

5

5 RULES FOR SETTING BOUNDARIES CLEARLY LAID OUT IN SCRIPTURE

So far we've looked to God's example in Scripture to guide us in our understanding of Biblical boundaries. As we've discovered, there is much to learn from His example!

But there are some things about boundaries He just comes right out and tells us. When it comes to these principles, we don't have to guess at all, or draw parallels with how He acts. In these areas, He spells it out plainly. We are simply left with the choice to listen and obey, or to ignore Him and do our own thing.

So let's look at 5 rules the Bible gives us for setting boundaries in our relationships:

Rule 1
We Reap What We Sow.

Proverbs 19:19
Hot-tempered people must pay the penalty. If you rescue them once, you will have to do it again.

2 Thessalonians 3:10
Even while we were with you, we gave you this command: "Those unwilling to work will not get to eat."

Galatians 6:7-8
Don't be misled – you cannot mock the justice of God. You will always harvest what you plant. Those who live only to satisfy their own sinful nature will harvest decay and death from that sinful nature. But those who live to please the Spirit will harvest everlasting life from the Spirit.

Oftentimes when we refuse to set boundaries it's because we don't want to see the people we love hurting. We get in between them and the natural consequences for their bad choices in an attempt to protect them. Unfortunately, what we're doing is the exact opposite of protection. Love does not participate in, or even enable sin.

Strong, Biblical boundaries keep us from becoming a party to things that do not please God, while at the same time allowing the misery that follows disobedience to fall squarely upon the one who has rebelled.

> Can you see how refusing to separate yourself from the sin of another has caused you to reap what was meant for them? Can you see how this may hurt them and their chances of recovery?

I was particularly struck by Galatians 6:7-8 that says, "you cannot mock the justice of God."

When I refuse to enact Biblical boundaries, I am attempting to mock the justice of God! I'm trying to stop the decay and death that is sure to grow from the scattered seeds of sin from sprouting.

What folly! For it is that very decay and death that is most likely to bring about the Godly sorrow that leads to repentance! It is the hunger that results from laziness that will drive the sluggard to work!

May God give us the courage to firmly establish our borders and get out of His way. May we have the strength to leave those who choose to wander outside to the consequences of their choices and remain safe within our walls.

DIG INTO SCRIPTURE

Find as many verses as you can that deal with the "justice of God." What do you learn from them?

------ Rule 2 ------
We Measure Actions, Not Words.

----

1 John 4:1
Dear friends, do not believe everyone who claims to speak by the Spirit. You must test them to see if the spirit they have comes from God. For there are many false prophets in the world.

John 3: 3 & 18-21
Jesus replied, "I tell you the truth, unless you are born again, you cannot see the Kingdom of God.... There is no judgment against anyone who believes in Him. But anyone who does not believe in Him has already been judged for not believing in God's one and only Son. And the judgment is based on this fact: God's light came into the world, but people loved the darkness more than the light, for their actions were evil. All who do evil hate the light and refuse to go near it for fear their sins will be exposed. But those who do what is right come to the light so others can see that they are doing what God wants."

Boundaries are violated by actions, and the gate back in should only be unlocked and opened as a result of actions as well.

> Have you ever found yourself confused when someone you loved claimed to be in a place that his actions didn't back up? What did you choose to trust? Words, or actions? Why?
>
> _____
> _____
> _____
> _____
> _____

In chapter 3 we talked about how God made a way through the blood of Jesus for us to get back to Him once we had violated His boundaries. (As we all have and do.) But that way is only open when we repent and in faith accept His gift.

Without the act of repentance there is no redemption.

We need to follow this example. But unlike God, we can't see a person's heart to know if repentance is true, simply because the offender says so. Words can be false, and the enemy is a master of deception. But the Bible tells us that evil will run from light, while righteousness will boldly step into the light for all to see.

Actions matter. We must become students of these actions.

DIG INTO SCRIPTURE
Read Galatians 5 and list below the fruit of the Spirit. How can we use these indicators to measure the actions of others?

_____
_____
_____
_____
_____
_____
_____
_____
_____

Strong Biblical boundaries will patiently and lovingly wait for
violators to step out into the light of Scripture –
willingly allowing their actions to come under scrutiny in order to
prove their genuine repentance.

And one who is truly repentant will be equally patient –
understanding time is needed and they have forfeited all rights.
Repentant violators understand that the gate is an act of grace – they
don't deserve it. So they will be willing to wait as long as they need to
for it to open.

------ Rule 3 ------
Make them with Confidence – It Will Hurt, but there Should be No Guilt in Obedience..

----

2 Corinthians 7:8-9
I am not sorry that I sent that severe letter to you, though I was sorry at first, for I know it was painful to you for a little while. Now I am glad I sent it, not because it hurt you, but because the pain caused you to repent and change your ways. It was the kind of sorrow God wants His people to have, so you were not harmed by us in any way. For the kind of sorrow God wants us to experience leads us away from sin and results in salvation. There's no regret for that kind of sorrow. But worldly sorrow, which lacks repentance, results in spiritual death.

The fact of the matter is, enforcing strong Biblical boundaries will
inevitably hurt people we love. Though really it is their own
sin hurting them, not the boundary. It just won't feel that way at first.

Likewise, watching people we love be hurt (seemingly) by our
boundaries will hurt us, and we will be tempted to feel sorry we
decided to act in obedience to God. But this is when it's so important
we understand this concept from a Biblical perspective!

We haven't set our boundaries to be mean. We haven't done it to punish or get revenge.

Our boundaries are to protect us from the consequences of another's sins, and to allow the full force of those consequences to fall on him – hopefully leading him to Godly sorrow which leads to repentance.

Biblical boundaries are an act of love!

> Have you ever made a boundary, only to later give in and fail to follow through with what you've said you'll do because you felt too bad or guilty when it came time to enforce the consequences? _____
> What was the driving force behind your guilt?
> _____
> _____
> _____
>
> Have you ever been talked out of enforcing a boundary by the trespassing person because they accused you of being mean or controlling? _____
> Looking back, were you actually being mean or controlling?
> _____
>
> Do you think these were healthy reactions? Why or why not?
> _____
> _____
> _____
> _____
> _____
> _____
> _____

------ Rule 4 ------
The Church Should Encourage and Support the Enforcement of Biblical Boundaries.

Matthew 18:15-20
If another believer sins against you, go privately and point out the offense. If the other person listens and confesses it, you have won that person back. But if you are unsuccessful, take one or two others with you and go back again, so that everything you say may be confirmed by two or three witnesses. If the person still refuses to listen, take your case to the church. Then if he or she won't accept the church's decision, treat that person as a pagan or a corrupt tax collector.
I tell you the truth, whatever you forbid on earth will be forbidden in heaven, and whatever you permit on earth will be permitted in heaven.
I also tell you this: If two of you agree here on earth concerning anything you ask, my Father in heaven will do it for you. For where two or three gather together as my followers, I am there among them.

What power we are missing out on in this New Testament Church Age by disregarding the need for strong boundaries in regards to sin amongst our members!

Bear with me for a bit, while I remind you of something that happened in the Old Testament era:
When God gave the law to Moses and the people of Israel, there were several lines He drew that were extremely rigid. For instance, in Deuteronomy 13 God demanded that the people of Israel put to death anyone who tried to entice others to worship other gods. He told them they had to "purge the evil from among them."

And this wasn't the only time He gave a command like that either. God had chosen these people to be set apart for Him. He intended for them to be a holy people.

But the Israelites didn't take those commands as seriously as God did. They did not enforce the consequences He had demanded for the broken boundaries. As a result, over time the hearts of the entire nation were turned from God.

The wickedness they had left unchecked festered and grew until it had taken over the hearts of all the people. They abandoned Him to the point He was forced to separate Himself from them for a time and send them into exile.

I ask you, church, have we not learned our lesson from them? When God sent Jesus to die for us, He grafted us into the nation of Israel and set us apart as His very own possession. A holy people. Yet we dare to minimize His commands to remain set apart!

I assert that the rampant corruption particularly in the area of sexual purity among the body of Christ is due in large part to our disobedience in this area! It should never be left to a wife alone to enforce strong Biblical boundaries with a husband who is unrepentantly unfaithful. (Pornography is cheating!)

The Bible has clearly laid out a procedure to follow in such cases, and not just in one place either! Let's not forget what we already read from 1 Corinthians 5! I know I already included the whole chapter on page 25, but since it is so important when dealing with Biblical boundaries, I'm going to include it again:

1 Corinthians 5
I can hardly believe the report about the sexual immorality going on among you – something that even pagans don't do... You are so proud of yourselves, but you should be mourning in sorrow and shame. And you should remove this man from your fellowship.

Even though I am not with you in person, I am with you in Spirit. And as though I were there, I have already passed judgement on this man in the name of the Lord Jesus. You must call a meeting of the church. I will be present with you in spirit, and so will the power of our Lord Jesus. Then you must throw this man out and hand him over to Satan so that his sinful nature will be destroyed and he himself will be saved on the day the Lord returns.
Your boasting about this is terrible. Don't you realize that this sin is like a little yeast that spreads through the whole batch of dough? Get rid of the old "yeast" by removing this wicked person from among you. Then you will be like a fresh batch of dough made without yeast, which is what you really are. Christ, our Passover Lamb, has been sacrificed for us. So let us celebrate the festival, not with the old bread of wickedness and evil, but with the new bread of sincerity and truth.
When I wrote to you before, I told you not to associate with people who indulge in sexual sin. But I wasn't talking about unbelievers who indulge in sexual sin, or are greedy, or cheat people, or worship idols. You would have to leave this world to avoid people like that. I meant that you are not to associate with anyone who claims to be a believer yet indulges in sexual sin, or is greedy, or worships idols, or is abusive, or is a drunkard, or cheats people. Don't even eat with such people.
It isn't my responsibility to judge outsiders, but it certainly is your responsibility to judge those inside the church who are sinning. God will judge those on the outside; but as the Scriptures say, You must remove the evil person from among you."

People of God, it is time to be obedient! Let it not be just a few of us who have the courage to obey – like Caleb and Joshua on the border of the Promised Land! Let us rise up as a body and put our faith in God – allowing HIM to handle the fall out of our obedience!

------ Rule 5 ------
Boundaries that Haven't been Communicated Clearly Should Never be Enforced.

Deuteronomy 29:29
The Lord our God has secrets known to no one. We are not accountable for them, but we and our children are accountable forever for all that He has revealed to us, so that we may obey all the terms of these instructions.

Our God is complex beyond anything we can even begin to imagine! He has revealed much of Himself to us through Scripture, but there is so much more about Him we don't know.

The Bible makes it clear – He won't hold us accountable for not knowing what He hasn't revealed to us. He does not expect us to read His mind. He DOES expect us to read His Word, and to live in obedience to it.

It is imperative we follow His example when setting up boundaries. Sisters, we are created in the image of our Lord – complex beyond the understanding of those around us. We absolutely cannot expect anyone to read our minds or anticipate our wants and needs. We HAVE to communicate them. And we cannot hold anyone accountable for what has not been communicated.

> Has anyone ever gotten upset with you because you failed to do something he believed you should have "just known" to do?
>
> _____
>
> How did that make you feel?
>
> _____
> _____

By the same token, the people in our lives are also created in the image of God – complex beyond our understanding. We cannot read their minds either. Nor can we expect to (or be expected to) anticipate their wants, needs, thoughts, motivations, etc…

Communication is imperative. No relationship can hope to be healthy without it.

> Would you say the communication in your relationship is strong, or weak? _____
> What are the main areas in which you need to work on improving it?
>
> _____
> _____
> _____
> _____
> _____
>
> Have you been guilty of expecting people to know what has not been clearly communicated? _____
> What are a few things you can commit to doing that will help?
>
> _____
> _____
> _____
> _____

Let's follow the example of our Lord, and the guidelines He has clearly set for us in Scripture! Let's clearly communicate our boundaries, and then let's expect that our terms be respected and upheld. Let's do our part to operate with integrity. Let's be who we've said we would be and do what we've said we would do.

6

HOW DO I SET BIBLICAL BOUNDARIES?
5 STEPS TO GET YOU STARTED

We've learned a lot about what the Bible has to say about boundaries. Now it's time to take what we've learned and figure out how to practically apply it. Let's answer the question, "How do I actually set Biblical boundaries?"

It's time to come up with a strategy for laying out our borders, building our fences, and installing our gates. First things first – let's remember how we defined a boundary in chapter one:

We cannot be cities with broken down walls anymore. It's time to take control of ourselves. It's time to stop being defined by someone

> PERSONAL BOUNDARIES DRAW A LINE OR FIX A LIMIT. THEY CLEARLY COMMUNICATE WHERE THE ACTIONS OF ANOTHER WILL REACH THE EXTENT OF OUR TOLERANCE AND THUS DIVIDE THEM FROM US. THEY DEFINE OUR BORDERS – WHO WE ARE. WHERE WE BEGIN, AND WHERE WE END.

else. It's time to let our actions be our own and choose obedience to God.

------ Setting Boundaries Step 1 ------
Define Yourself

We've already dealt with this issue quite a bit in chapter four. If you're still struggling to find your identity in Christ, the book of Ephesians offers so much wisdom on identity. Take some time this week and read it. It's short. 6 chapters. Read one each day. Write down everything you see about who you are, what you've been given in Christ, what God has asked of you, and what power you have in Him.

DIG INTO SCRIPTURE

Who I Am:

What I've been Given in Christ:

What God has Asked of Me:

What Power I have in Christ:

In the meantime, let's look at this passage in 1 Peter:

1 Peter 2:9-10
...You are a chosen people. You are royal priests, a holy nation, God's very own possession. As a result, you can show others the goodness of God, for He called you out of the darkness into His wonderful light. "Once you had no identity as a people; now you are God's people. Once you received no mercy; now you have received God's mercy."

According to the Bible, we are defined as this:
-God's very own possession. Chosen by Him!
-We have been called out of darkness so that we can live in the light.
-We have been set apart.

We must begin to lay our borders in such a way as to only allow in what will keep us in that place of holiness.

Our model is God. We've spent plenty of time establishing how He lays His boundaries. He sets standards. Those who violate those standards are given the freedom to do so, but they will also not be allowed into His house in that state.

As we begin to craft our walls let's answer these questions:

QUESTION 1: HOW DOES GOD DEFINE ME?

QUESTION 2: WHAT STANDARDS SHOULD I HAVE BECAUSE OF WHO GOD HAS CALLED ME TO BE?

QUESTION 3: WHAT SPECIFIC ACTIONS ARE VIOLATING THAT STANDARD GOD HAS SET ABOUT WHO I AM?

1 John 2:15-16
Do not love this world nor the things it offers you, for when you love the world, you do not have the love of the Father in you. For the world offers only a craving for physical pleasure, a craving for everything we see, and pride in our achievements and possessions. These are not from the Father, but are from this world.

Let's be sure we're committed to being wholly devoted to God! Let's not get caught up in a love for the things of this world – not even when those things are people or relationships that are not pleasing or honoring to God. Let's make His standards our standards. Always!

------ Setting Boundaries Step 2 ------
Define Your Responsibility

This can be a complicated topic for believers. The Bible can seem a bit contradictory, but the truth is, what we need is discernment.

We are called to help one another, but we are not called to be responsible for the conduct of another.

We have to figure out what parts of the situation we can take responsibility for, and what parts we cannot.

Galatians 6:1-2
Dear brothers and sisters, if another believer is overcome by some sin, you who are godly should gently and humbly help that person back onto the right path. And be careful not to fall into the same temptation yourself. Share each other's burdens, and in this way obey the law of Christ.

Galatians 6:4-5
Pay careful attention to your own work, for then you will get the satisfaction of a job well done, and you won't need to compare yourself to anyone else. For we are each responsible for our own conduct.

QUESTION 1: WHAT ARE SOME THINGS I KNOW I AM RESPONSIBLE FOR IN THIS RELATIONSHIP?

QUESTION 2: WHAT ARE SOME THINGS I KNOW I AM NOT RESPONSIBLE FOR IN THIS RELATIONSHIP?

QUESTION 3: WHAT ARE A FEW STANDARDS I CAN SET THAT ENCOMPASS MY RESPONSIBILITY, BUT DON'T TRY TO CONTROL WHAT IS NOT MY RESPONSIBILITY?

------ Setting Boundaries Step 3 ------
Check Your Motives and Ask for Wisdom

Once we've established who we are and what our responsibilities are, we have to take a step back and establish exactly what our goals are in drawing those lines.

In other words, we need to do a quick motives check. As we do, it would serve us well to also take a second to ask God for His wisdom as we move forward. Ask Him to reveal anything in us that falls out of line with His will.

This step is to ensure that we're not setting up our perimeter to manipulate or control someone else, but to genuinely protect both ourselves and those we love. That is the purpose of a good boundary – to protect.

This step will also help equip us to clearly and concisely communicate our boundaries when we get to that step.

Proverbs 27:5-6
An open rebuke is better than hidden love! Wounds from a sincere friend are better than many kisses from an enemy.
Colossians 4:5-6
Live wisely among those who are not believers, and make the most of every opportunity. Let your conversation be gracious and attractive so that you will have the right response for everyone.

QUESTION 1: WHAT DO I HOPE WILL BE THE RESULT OF SETTING THIS BOUNDARY?

QUESTION 2: IS THAT GOAL HONORING TO GOD?

QUESTION 3: WHAT ARE SOME OTHER POSSIBLE RESULTS OF SETTING THIS BOUNDARY?

QUESTION 4: HOW DO THOSE POSSIBILITIES MAKE ME FEEL?

QUESTION 5: WHAT IS GOD ASKING ME TO DO IN THIS AREA?

QUESTION 6: AFTER EVALUATING MY MOTIVES, DO I FEEL THIS BOUNDARY CAN BE MADE WITH INTEGRITY AND IN OBEDIENCE TO GOD?

------ Setting Boundaries Step 4 ------
Choose Consequences and Install Your Gate

This is a difficult step, but if we've done the work of the previous steps, we can proceed with confidence.

We know who we are. We know what we're responsible for. We know our motives. And we know what God is asking us to do. Now, we just have to build that fence to keep out what doesn't belong, and install a gate.

Keep in mind, a gate works two ways. It provides a way for us to send out what doesn't belong and offers a way back in for those on the outside.

Remember too what we learned in Chapter 5 – The purpose of the consequence to a boundary is to allow others to reap what they sow.

Galatians 6:7-8
Don't be misled – you cannot mock the justice of God. You will always harvest what you plant. Those who live only to satisfy their own sinful nature will harvest decay and death from that sinful nature. But those who live to please the Spirit will harvest everlasting life from the Spirit.

QUESTION 1: WHAT IS THE NATURAL CONSEQUENCE OF THE OFFENDING BEHAVIOR?

QUESTION 2: WHAT ACTIONS CAN I TAKE TO GET OUT OF THE WAY OF THOSE CONSEQUENCES AND ALLOW THEM TO LAND SQUARELY ON THE ONE WHO IS BREAKING THE ESTABLISHED STANDARD?

QUESTION 3: DOES THIS CONSEQUENCE ATTEMPT TO TAKE JUSTICE INTO MY OWN HANDS IN ORDER TO SEEK REVENGE? OR DOES IT LEAVE JUSTICE IN GOD'S VERY CAPABLE HANDS?

QUESTION 4: ARE MY PARAMETERS CLEAR? CAN I EASILY COMMUNICATE WHAT MY ACTIONS WILL BE IN A WAY THAT LEAVES NO ROOM FOR QUESTIONS OR MANIPULATION?

Now that our gate swings out, let's provide a way back in too.

QUESTION 5: WHAT ACTIONS WILL PROVE TO ME THAT THERE HAS BEEN A HEART-CHANGE?

QUESTION 6: WHAT ARE SOME CLEAR STEPS THAT CAN BE TAKEN TO RESTORE THE RELATIONSHIP?

QUESTION 7: CAN I CLEARLY COMMUNICATE THESE STEPS IN A WAY THAT LEAVES NO ROOM FOR QUESTIONS OR MANIPULATION?

------ Setting Boundaries Step 5 ------
Clearly and Concisely Communicate Your Boundaries

All that's left now is to write out exactly what you've come up with.

- WRITE YOUR BOUNDARY

- WRITE YOUR REASON

- WRITE YOUR CONSEQUENCE

- WRITE THE WAY BACK IN

Be clear. Put time frames on it. Once it's all written out, present it verbally and also in writing at the same time. Give an opportunity for questions, but don't allow yourself to be manipulated. Stand firm sister. You've taken the time to seek God in this. You've taken the time to align yourself to His Word. Stand firm! Be obedient. Don't back down! Remember:

Proverbs 25:28
A person without self-control is like a city with broken-down walls.

7

SETTING BOUNDARIES WORKSHEET

*Additional Copies of this worksheet can be found on the website: hisdearlyloveddaughter.com if you would like to have one for multiple boundaries.

Identify the Problem:

Before you can ask the questions we talked about in the last chapter, you have to identify the problem.

What is a specific behavior, attitude, or action that makes you feel violated or unsafe? (Be as specific as possible)

_____
_____
_____
_____
_____
_____

Now let's answer the questions from the previous chapter using only the issue you've identified here.

Step 1 – Define Yourself

1. How has God defined me when it comes to this area? What does the Bible say about it?

   _____
   _____
   _____
   _____
   _____
   _____

2. What standards should I have in this area because of who God has called me to be?

   _____
   _____
   _____
   _____
   _____

3. What specific actions are violating this standard God has set about who I am?

   _____
   _____
   _____
   _____
   _____

Step 2 – Define Your Responsibility

1. When it comes to this issue, what are some things I know I AM responsible for in this relationship?

   _____
   _____
   _____
   _____

2. What are some things I know I AM NOT responsible for in this relationship?

   _____
   _____
   _____
   _____

3. What are a few standards I can set that encompass my responsibility, but don't try to control what is not my responsibility?

   _____
   _____
   _____
   _____
   _____
   _____

Step 3 – Check Your Motives and Ask for Wisdom

1. What is the specific result I'm hoping for as a result of setting a boundary in this area?

   _____
   _____
   _____
   _____

2. Is that goal honoring to God? _____

3. If I'm being realistic, what are some other possible results of setting a boundary in this area?

   _____
   _____
   _____
   _____
   _____

4. How does it make me feel when I think about those possibilities?

   _____
   _____
   _____
   _____
   _____

5. Regardless of how I *feel*, what is God asking me to do in this area?

_____

_____

_____

_____

6. After evaluating my motives, do I feel like there is a boundary I need to set in this area that can be made with integrity and in obedience to God?

_____

_____

_____

_____

Step 4 – Choose Your Consequences and Install Your Gate

1. Are there any natural consequences to the behavior that's causing a problem in this area? (If so, what are they, and have I been getting in the way of those consequences?)

_____

_____

_____

_____

_____

2. What actions can I take to get out of the way of the consequences and allow them to land squarely on the one who is breaking the established standard?

3. Does the consequence I've named attempt to take justice into my own hands in order to seek revenge? Or does it leave justice in God's very capable hands?

4. Can I clearly lay out my parameters? Can I clearly communicate what my actions will be in a way that leaves no room for questions or manipulations? _____
Name the parameters and actions:

5. If the boundary is broken, what actions will then prove to me there has been a heart-change?

6. What are some clear steps that can be taken by the offender at that point to restore the relationship?

7. Can I clearly communicate these steps in a way that leaves no room for questions or manipulations? _____
Name the steps:

Step 5 – Clearly and Concisely Communicate Your Boundary

1. Write your boundary:

2. Write your reason:

3. Write your consequence:

4. Write the way back in:

8

EXAMPLE WORKSHEET

*This is the same worksheet found in the previous chapter filled out with a boundary Esther has established in her marriage for you to use as an example. Hopefully this will make it very simple to understand what a Biblical boundary looks like, and how the worksheet can help you lay it out.

Identify the Problem:

Before you can ask the questions we talked about in the last chapter, you have to identify the problem.

What is a specific behavior, attitude, or action that makes you feel violated or unsafe? (Be as specific as possible)

Being lied to. When I am lied to it causes me to question everything about our lives. I begin to wonder if there is anything I can trust at all. I have been lied to so many times, it has become difficult to know how to interpret my reality.

Now let's answer the questions from the previous chapter using only the issue you've identified here.

Step 1 – Define Yourself

1. How has God defined me when it comes to this area? What does the Bible say about it?

   <u>According to Proverbs 6:16-17, Proverbs 12:22, Psalms 5:6, and many other passages, God hates a lying tongue. And according to Ephesians 5, I should imitate God. As a daughter of the Lord, I should have a big problem with lies</u>

2. What standards should I have in this area because of who God has called me to be?

   <u>God makes strong boundaries around being lied to in Scripture and so should I. I should not ever knowingly tolerate being lied to</u>

3. What specific actions are violating this standard God has set about who I am?

   <u>When my husband is active in his addiction, lies become a part of his regular behavior. He lies about anything. Sometimes just for the sake of lying. I do not believe lies are part of a healthy relationship</u>

Step 2 – Define Your Responsibility

4. When it comes to this issue, what are some things I know I AM responsible for in this relationship?

I am responsible for what I do with the truth when it is revealed to me. I am responsible for setting standards that make it clear I will not tolerate being lied to. I am responsible to tell the truth myself, no matter what.

5. What are some things I know I AM NOT responsible for in this relationship?
I can not make my husband tell the truth and am not responsible for his actions. But I can trust God to reveal truth to me. I'm not responsible for how my husband responds to my boundaries once I set them in place.

6. What are a few standards I can set that encompass my responsibility, but don't try to control what is not my responsibility?
I can set standards that set out what I will do if I discover I have been lied to. I can regularly pray verses like Luke 8:17, asking God to reveal what has been hidden from me.

Step 3 – Check Your Motives and Ask for Wisdom

7. What is the specific result I'm hoping for as a result of setting a boundary in this area?
I hope my husband will realize that telling lies is unacceptable and that

nothing good comes from it. I hope he'll realize he can't get away with it because God always reveals the truth. I hope he'll have a heart change and decide to live a life of truth before God and man.

8. Is that goal honoring to God? Yes. Honoring and trusting Him.

9. If I'm being realistic, what are some other possible results of setting a boundary in this area?
He could become angry, or even bitter that he is being held to a standard he doesn't have any interest in conforming to and choose to leave this relationship and pursue divorce.

10. How does it make me feel when I think about those possibilities?
Really sad, really scared, and if I'm honest a little angry. This is not a crazy ask! It should be a no-brainer in marriage.

11. Regardless of how I *feel*, what is God asking me to do in this area?
Set a strong boundary around the truthfulness of our relationship. He wants me to be committed to truth. And He wants me to trust Him with the results.

12. After evaluating my motives, do I feel like there is a boundary I need to set in this area that can be made with integrity and in obedience to God?

Yes I need to put my foot down and stop tolerating lies in our relationship

Step 4 – Choose Your Consequences and Install Your Gate

13. Are there any natural consequences to the behavior that's causing a problem in this area? (If so, what are they, and have I been getting in the way of those consequences?)
    The natural consequence of lying is lost trust and broken relationship

14. What actions can I take to get out of the way of the consequences and allow them to land squarely on the one who is breaking the established standard?
    I can stop going on with life like everything is normal when I find out I'm being lied to again, and instead ask him to leave the house for a time. I can stop covering for him by not letting anyone else know what a liar he is. I can insist that trust be rebuilt by consistent truth-telling before I agree to re-establish normalcy in the relationship.

15. Does the consequence I've named attempt to take justice into my own hands in order to seek revenge? Or does it leave justice in God's very capable hands?
    I think it leaves justice in God's hands. I will not be going out of my way to tell everyone what he has done or act aggressively towards him. I will

simply remove myself from his influence, stop hiding, and let him answer for his own behavior.

16. Can I clearly lay out my parameters? Can I clearly communicate what my actions will be in a way that leaves no room for questions or manipulations? Yes
    Name the parameters and actions: He will have 24 hours to tell me anything I need to know. After that, it will be considered a lie. If/when I find out I have been lied to I will separate myself from him for a minimum of 30 days.

17. If the boundary is broken, what actions will then prove to me there has been a heart-change?
    I will need to see consistent truth-telling. Also, I will need to see total cooperation with my boundaries. It will need to be done with humility and remorse. Otherwise I will know there is no true repentance and the relationship will be over.

18. What are some clear steps that can be taken by the offender at that point to restore the relationship?
    He can willingly leave the house for the 30 days and place himself in a safe place during that time. He can communicate his remorse. He can

check in with me daily on his own, taking that opportunity to tell me as much truth as he can think of.

19. Can I clearly communicate these steps in a way that leaves no room for questions or manipulations? Yes (See above)

Step 5 – Clearly and Concisely Communicate Your Boundary

Write your boundary:
I am drawing a hard line in the sand around my willingness to abide with lies. I will no longer just put up with being lied to. From now on you have 24 hours to tell me the truth about anything I need to know. After that, if I find out you have kept something from me, or directly lied about something to me you will be in violation of my boundary.

4. Write your reason:
God makes it clear in Scripture that He detests lies, and as His daughter, so do I. Your lies have shattered my trust and ruined our relationship. I will not be a part of a relationship anymore that is so displeasing to God. I will tell the truth, and I expect to be told the truth from now on.

5. Write your consequence:

I will ask you to leave our house for at least 30 days in order to spend time earning back my trust from a safe distance. If you won't leave, I will. And I will take the kids with me. At the end of the 30 days I will re-evaluate what I believe God is asking of me at that point.

Write the way back in:

While you are living somewhere else (somewhere safe like your parent's house, or with a trusted Christian family member/friend) you will be free to communicate with me, and if you want to rebuild trust you will take the opportunity to work on telling the truth with daily check-ins. You will need to find a way to prove to me that you are taking truth-telling seriously and that you understand what a violation of God's standard it is to lie. I will need to believe you understand how damaging your lies have been. I need to know you are committed to living in truth, and that you have truly repented. I will be counting on God to show me this. And you'll just have to accept what I tell you God is telling me on the subject. A bad attitude about this will prove to me that you aren't repentant.

9

HOW BIBLICAL BOUNDARIES PUT GOD IN CONTROL

Before we wrap this up, let's take the time to remind ourselves of who's in control. What it's so easy to forget in the midst of all the chaos of life is that being obedient to God in this area (really in any area) allows us to step out of the way and Him to do His work. It puts God in control!

If you remember, when we started this study, we talked about how God established boundaries right from the beginning. When he placed Adam in the garden of Eden He told him not to eat the fruit from the tree of the Knowledge of Good and Evil. He also told him the consequences – if you do, you will surely die.

Of course, we all know how the story goes – Eve was deceived by Satan and ate the fruit and gave some to Adam who also ate the fruit. It's possible the only reason Adam ate it was because he was afraid of being separated from Eve if he chose obedience when she did not. But let's think about that possibility for a second.

Do we really believe God wouldn't have provided for Adam in that situation?

It seems obvious in that scenario that obedience would have resulted in provision and great reward. So why do we doubt our God will do the same for us? Why do we allow the fear of lost relationship, or a lack of provision to keep us from obedience?

The thing is, when God showed up in the Garden and asked what happened everyone started playing the blame game. Adam blamed Eve, and Eve blamed the serpent. But in verses 14-24 of the third chapter of Genesis God handed out consequences to each according to his or her own sin. It didn't matter what anyone else had done. Adam was responsible for Adam, Eve was responsible for Eve, and Satan was responsible for Satan.

> What are the implications for us in how God held each member of the garden story responsible for his/her own behavior?
> _____
> _____
> _____
> _____

Afterward, God set up new boundaries. Ones that kept people out of the garden forever in order to ensure they wouldn't be able to eat the fruit from the tree of life and be stuck forever in a state of corruption and separation from Him.

He began right then enacting a plan that would offer a way back into right relationship with Him forever.

That is the God we serve my friends! A God of boundaries, but for one very important reason: To protect us.

Because He loves us.

The system He has set up does not allow any of us to take on the responsibility for the sins of another. We are accountable only for our own actions. At the same time, in order to avoid being caught up in the sins of another, we absolutely must separate ourselves from them. We must be set apart for our Lord!

Strong, healthy, Biblical boundaries stop the cycle of blaming others for our situations. They make the statement that we are taking responsibility for ourselves, and trusting God to take care of us - that we are choosing obedience, whether others choose to join us in that decision or not.

Can we be resolved to do this? Can we allow God to be in control? Can we leave our loved ones in His hands and allow Him to call them out of their sorrowful state and into His glorious light in His own way and in His own time? Do we trust Him enough to be obedient?

> What are you most afraid will happen if you stop making excuses about why you "can't" make boundaries?
> _____
> _____
> _____
>
> What are you most afraid will happen if you get out of God's way and allow His judgment to fall on the people you love?
> _____
> _____
> _____
>
> Do you really believe your efforts outside of God's biblical standards are changing anything for the better?
> _____
> _____
> _____

Whatever control we're trying to hang onto – it is an illusion! Let's choose obedience! Let's set and keep boundaries that bring honor to God.

Let's be set apart.

Holy.

Let's let God be in control!

And finally, let's remember that if we're still breathing, our story isn't over yet. Just because it looks dark and hopeless today does not mean it will end that way! Let's remain faithful and trust our tomorrows to HIM!

Ecclesiastes 3:1-8
For everything there is a season, a time for every activity under heaven. A time to be born and a time to die. A time to plant and a time to harvest. A time to kill and a time to heal. A time to tear down and a time to build up. A time to cry and a time to laugh. A time to grieve and a time to dance. A time to scatter stones and a time to gather stones. A time to embrace and a time to turn away. A time to search and a time to quit searching. A time to keep and a time to throw away. A time to tear and a time to mend. A time to be quiet and a time to speak. A time to love and a time to hate. A time for war and a time for peace.

10

A PRAYER FOR HELP

Heavenly Father,

Thank-you that You are a God of boundaries. Thank-you for not creating a world of chaos and confusion, but one of order and righteous standards. Thank-you that You are good, and holy, and our perfect example. Thank-you that You're in control and not us. We're trusting YOU! Help us to be obedient.

Father, we are asking You for wisdom. As we commit to the study of Your Word, give us eyes to see, ears to hear, hearts that understand, and feet that are quick to obey! Give us faith to believe what you say, and the trust to wholly commit to you all of our ways.

Remind us daily of Your unfailing love so that our confidence in You and Your sovereignty will grow. Reassure us of Your grace and mercy. Help us to place those we love into Your hands and leave them there trusting you to take care of both us and them.

As we spend time searching Your Word for truth, Father, give us wisdom and understanding and the courage to obey. In Jesus's Name, amen!

References

Merriam-Webster, Incorporated, 2018. Definition of "boundary". https://www.merriam-webster.com/dictionary/boundary

Oxford University Press, 2018. Definition of "boundary". https://en.oxforddictionaries.com/definition/boundary

Unless otherwise indicated, all Scripture quotations are taken from the Holy Bible, New Living Translation, copyright © 1996, 2004, 2007 by Tyndale House Foundation. Used by permission of Tyndale House Publishers, Inc., Carol Stream, Illinois 60188. All rights reserved.

ABOUT THE AUTHOR

Esther Hosea is the pen name of Cherith Peters, the founder of His Dearly Loved Daughter Ministries. In 2017, shortly after discovering the extent of her husband's sexual addiction and chronic unfaithfulness, Cherith began writing under the name Esther Hosea at the blog hisdearlyloveddaughter.com.

In the years that followed God began working miracles and moving mountains. Not only did He set her husband free from his addiction, but He also began the work of restoring and rebuilding their marriage into something truly beautiful.

Out of the ashes of addiction's destruction He raised an entire ministry dedicated to fighting the battles waged by the enemy in the area of sexual purity in marriage. Women and men all over the world have found help and healing through the God of Esther's story. Truly, He has created her for such a time as this!

May every ounce of glory be given to Him!

Made in the USA
Columbia, SC
30 January 2022